ASYLUM

2000 Agnes Lynch Starrett Poetry Prize

PITT POETRY SERIES
Ed Ochester, Editor

Asylum

Quan Barry

UNIVERSITY OF
PITTSBURGH PRESS

PENNSYLVANIA
COUNCIL
ON THE

The publication of this book is supported by a grant from the
Pennsylvania Council on the Arts

Published by the University of Pittsburgh Press, Pittsburgh, Pa., 15261
Manufactured in the United States of America
Printed on acid-free paper
10 9 8 7 6 5 4 3 2 1

ISBN 0-8229-5769-8

for my parents Tom and Ingrid Barry—
with love and laughter

CONTENTS

ASYLUM

I've lain with the devil,
cursed God above,
forsaken heaven
to bring you my love.

—P J Harvey

asylum

The fish are the first to return:
the moorish idol, the black surgeon,

the trumpet and lesser scorpion, the angel
seemingly radiogenic, the goatfish

with its face of spikes. Whole phyla converging:
the devil rays in fluid sheets, the leatherbacks,

hawksbills, their shells reticent as maps.
On the atoll: the golden plover, the kingfisher,

egrets and honeyeaters
nesting like an occupation. And the flowers:

the flame trees, the now forgotten, the wait-a-bit
all drawn to what we desert, a preserve

where the chinese lantern's elliptic seed
is bone-smooth, cesium-laced.

child of the enemy

I've seen thousands of Amerasians, and I have two Amerasian [children] of
my own. Amerasians are willful and stubborn. They have serious identity
problems. They have no discipline. Down the street at the Floating Hotel
you'll find Amerasian prostitutes plying their mothers' trade. I think there's
a racial thing here, something genetic.
—an American ex-soldier as quoted in *Vietnamerica*

I. NIGHT TERROR

It started when I was four.
Vacation. Door County, Wisconsin.
The alewives rippling on the rocks
like a flock of birds, the sudden knowledge
growing like a toll. Then
I couldn't have articulated it, but I knew.
It wasn't the beached fish that frightened me.
It was the ones that got away, far away
under the wreck of water. The ones that survived
by fleeing, kin left rotting on the shore.

II. TWENTY YEARS LATER

Someone who had been there
(and now incidentally is serving
a natural life sentence)

told you it wasn't all
about killing. *Don't ever believe
you weren't conceived in love.*

You take his word for it
like an imago splitting the shell,
each wet wing a voice

purged and steeling.

III. CHILD OF THE ENEMY

a.

I was born with a twelfth hole. Instantly
the floating world carved its shame
on the dark meat of my face. A love child, child of perfidy, allegiance
      split like a door.
I was born a traitor in the month of Cancer, the white phosphorus
pungent, knowing.

b.

1973. The rice winnows out like shrapnel. Before it's over
there are fifty thousand new hostilities, each birthed face inimical
as our fathers stealing home.

c.

Think of the places women dilate. Beds. Barns. Saigon's streets.
No good Samaritan comes forward and only the moon like a platoon
treacherously approaching, its extended hand like a speculum, the better
to illuminate, disgrace.

                    d.

              Or more importantly
the places women leave. An unsuspecting caretaker. The bacterial streets.
                    Or
           perhaps the unspeakable pitch into burlap
and water.   A gulf off the South China Sea where another sinking form
is anyone's guess.

e.

That time Tet fell in the year of the snake. As in reptilian. As in
no turning back. As in when I became
a child of containment. As in how like a monetary policy

I was loosed to an existence feral as a raised bayonet. As in
what the serpent might say: knowledge for knowledge's sake
is both industrial and complex.

f.

At birth
I was swaddled
in a blanket. Pink
wool. Threadbare.
Like everything else
moth-eaten.
Man-made.

g.

Before the last vertical bird lifted like a gurney out of April
and twenty years clotted to a tumor brilliant as a stuck fish
and the dreams began in which you saw yourself as the killer
of trees, before the army finally said it was something in the water
and orange came to be the cloak of mourning, tell me soldier:
who taught you to love like a man, you with nowhere to go
but tacitly free?

IV. THE EXILED

> I liked it in South Vietnam.
> —Lieutenant William Calley

Later   when the black
and white photos came in   the rice
sinking in its makeshift grave at the right
of the picture   three children wound
about their mother like meat on a spit   one eye
rolling loose   amazed   in the dead

silence of the frame   the freshly dead
posed hastily   each wound
breaking open like a smile   each eye
cocked as if winking under the black
hood of hair   the stalked rice
a backdrop   nobody wanted to write

the story   after all   no american in his right
mind would rise to this black
mission   109 civilians dead
    gunned down in the eye
of the hunt   it was never about them   the rice
lush in ways their children could never be   wound

so tightly to old wounds
    the chinese   the french   now this blue-eyed
christ seated at the right
of the throne   coming to save them from a black
plague that left so many dead
    rotting in fields like unharvested rice

this is where it began   in the rice
paddies of vietnam   my mother   her right
hand gripping the earth's black
pillow   the night bleeding like a wound
   the soldier digging into her with the dead
weight of his lust   every star an amazed eye

rolling loose in the night   nine months   i
had just one picture taken in saigon   my black
hair sprouting   toes wound
in knots   mouth like a fist   the rice
paper riddled with figures   my right
foot inked   marked like a prayer for the dead

listen   you don't know me   eyes wild as rice
   like wounds scarred black
lieutenant   if revenge is a rite of passage   i need you dead

V. OUR KAMIKAZE

semper fi

Next time they won't be crazy.

They won't stand in My Lai laughing at the split throats, the humid spring
pitted with shells.

They won't drop down on the darker places, a gun in each hand, beguiling:
Here and here. Come and live.

They won't cry out when the doors throw open and they stream like teeth
into the sky's blue yolk.

They won't forget the children, the undeveloped girls they seeded,
shredded.

They won't enter the cities on foot, arms outstretched
to bring the disciples their blood.

Later
they won't not have enough gas to make it back.

VI. FLASHBACK

Every night Achilles laid down to this: how he roped
the breaker of horses to his disfiguring wheel, Patroklos
a boy in wolf's clothing. Then
when the arrow in its thirst arrived, this hero,
tired of living in two worlds,
let it plant, forgiving seed et al.
If only my father could do the same.

VII. OBITUARY OF A BIOLOGICAL MOTHER

She was born upon a time.
In what became. The defoliated.

Congenital. Occidental. Out of order.
Everything. She knew she learned

from rape. Involvement
in lieu of war. In the bladed years. She conceived.

End of ever after.
End of happily.

She is survived by one. Who lives.
As though she were dead of childbirth. Consequently.

She must have. Done
some things right. Mother of a bastard.

Who died on whom.

(VIII. A CODA

Now belatedly
I see
the moon's dry surgings

for what they are.
Newton
believed the Bible

hides our names
in its pages, our deeds
printed like receipts.

I didn't know
I could need to know
like this,

the moon
cutting her indifferent
recessional. And you,

you,
my once-met,
tell me

who gave the world
free will?
Subsequently

who made
the fifth dimension
mercy?

It's rhetorical.
Mother, I never
didn't believe.)

IX. NAPALM

I have come to realize the body is its own pyre, that degree
rises from within, the fatty acids a kind of kindling.
Like a scientist in a lab, this much I have established, blood jelled
like gasoline, the years spread before me like a map
pinned with targets, where I'm raging even now.
It works both ways. Clear the forests to see your enemies
and your enemies see you clearly. Like all effective incendiaries,
I won't only bloom where I'm planted.

The Glimmer Man

"Seagal told acquaintances that he believed he had been a holy man in a
previous life."
—*Esquire*

"I'm not supposed to fight—it's against my religion."
—Steven Seagal in *The Glimmer Man*

He has a memory of begging, of shaving his scalp
    smooth as an alms bowl. On the fourth night,
        in the *dojo* behind his eyes, he waits for the songbird

        to visit him again, open the wheel. He believes he is found
    in the old ways—dreams, a shaman pitching silks
into a lake, waiting for the reflection to settle, disclose

where the soul replants its light. To him his last life
    explains much—the reed-like timbre of his voice
        whittled from the thin mountain air, his taste for black

        traced to his immolation in white. "I am a refuge
from the three worlds. My path is love." He receives
his title in the year of the wood bull, his one act

of choosing the dead man's conch proof enough
    to name him *revealer of treasures.* Cloaked in gold brocade, the joss
        sticks' fragrant sacrifice, his body shimmers quietly, illuminated

        by butter lamps sconced to the walls. A *tulku,*
    he knows from this life what the right role can do,
how some lights last only until push comes to shove.

If dy/dx=4x³ + x² - 12/ 2x ² - 9, then

you are standing at the ocean,
in the moon's empirical light
each mercurial wave

like a parabola shifting on its axis,
the sea's dunes differentiated & graphed.
If this, then that. The poet

laughs. She wants to lie
in her own equation, the point slope
like a woman whispering *stay me*

with flagons. What is it to know the absolute value
of negative grace, to calculate
how the heart becomes the empty set

uninteresectable, the first & the last?
But enough.
You are standing on the shore,

the parameters like wooden stakes.
Let X be the moon like a notary.
Let Y be all things left unsaid.

Let the constant be the gold earth
waiting to envelop what remains,
the sieves of the lungs like two cones.

intercellular aubade

inspired by *The Matrix*

As if the maker didn't know where to begin—
diastole or systole, the warring symmetry of closed circuits,

the zygote's rapid spoking into *other*.
Like everything that shoots grappling hooks, say

the lacewing with its compound eyes, its thousand thousand brood
oviposited to beat the odds. And for what?

A toehold? Dominance? For the right
to determine the helix, the how

things know to differentiate—
the fetal calf's multi-chambered stomach,

the distinctly cooling planets, the stars
zodiacal, seemingly white-hard? The why am I

I and not you? The reason we come into being?
O poor Tom! O flesh which bleeds air!

O how everything wants to generate something!
O there ain't no life nowhere! O judgment coursing

through each particle of an atom's weight!
O the sea's green platelets! O the sky's nitrogen grace!

intermurals

The first time my mother decided to come
somebody lost an eye. Almost, besides,
valedictorian, ivy league-bound, Lorie Ardiff had no right
being on the field, the fifteen fibrous seams
basting her eyelid together
a consequence of this. The second time
it was Zoë Burbridge who leaned into it, jumped back
like a dancer with the spirit, her cheekbone split,
fresh as an oyster. After that, my mother stayed home

four long years, not even trekking to the Berkshires, NESN
and the state championship where I made
that incomplete pass out of bounds, hands numb
with December, the ball hard as an explicated tumor, pillaging
free at last. She said she didn't spend the sixties
bra burning so her daughter could master the subtle art
of bloodletting in a kilt. *Suit yourself.* Like marijuana
field hockey led to harsher things—

lacrosse, two semesters of collegiate rugby
where I learned to take it like a man,
dish the dirt, wrap my arms around the enemy's knees
and snap, the contact inflicted with affection. It's only now
I remember the one who didn't get up, the girl
they carried off the field in a fireman's stretcher, leg cocked back
like a carbine. It goes without saying
that I was exultant, frenzied with the power
to cripple. Who wouldn't be?
All those years my mother stayed home
determined like a conscientious objector
to blow this wall tumbling down.

Job 42:4

Forget all you've seen,
bird, old woman, cage . . .
—Osip Mandelstam

Like a telegram
announcing your death
two months too late.

An exile
to the disaffecting—
the snow, the river

pouring endlessly
over your death-wound,
the cruel hinge.

Nights
the guards warm
vodka in their throats,

the Urals anonymous
like a tourniquet,
like famished hands,

like the blue flames
of corpses.
Where the silence goes on

like a horse
after the rider falls,
where man

is the only god,
you are manifold.
It is our right to ask.

kabuki

Why his father taught him to bite the corners of handkerchiefs, pout
as they had done for the last half millennium, his father's father and others
passing it to their sons—*onnagata*, woman-like—each generation perfecting it,
switching from lead-based paints that left them dumb to shellacking their eyes
with vermilion, ash superior for eyebrows, how a second honorific set
should sit just below the hairline, be applied by thumb as he was more woman
than a woman could be whose neck would snap like a *sakura* branch
under the sheen of a thirty pound wig, the cherry blossoms strewn
along the *hanamichi* where he makes her entrance, legs bound in the twenty *kimono*
she wears at once, this woman who asks nothing of love but the right to die,
damask robes cut to show her back glazed like porcelain as she manipulates
the ribs of her fan in the wisteria dance, taking the black silk in her mouth,
lips lacquered like butterflies, to keep from crying *onegai, onegai, onegai, please*
to an audience as captivated by her wanton passivity as I am because
I didn't know I could want one night of *koi* with a woman, perhaps any woman
so skilled in ruth.

Kaiserschmarn

Komm Herr Jesu, sei unser Gast,
Und segne was du uns bescheret hast.

With your paring knife
remove the rind from one small-sized lemon, then grate
the peel until its shavings coat your palm. Blend this
with enough white sugar until the mixture yellows
like the underbelly of a young hare in spring, then set aside.

Separate four eggs. Before cracking hold each above an open flame
to see that the yolk is unbloody and intact.
When you have satisfaction, break the shells
being careful to let each fluid fall at its own speed
distinctly. In a small glass bowl
beat the whites until they ridge, peak.
To hold the stiffness, add a pair of heavy pinches white sugar, beat again
then set aside.

In a large mixing bowl whisk your yolks until lemon-colored
or one shade past canary. Then, alternately,
stir in one fistful of flour, a half glass milk
until your batter is as pale as polished pine.
Using a wooden spoon, fold the egg whites into your mixture
as if you were folding satin on a bolt, doubling
the batter over and over on itself
until its consistency is uniform, ribbon-sleek.

Heat your skillet
to the same temperature you use for grouse.
Work one pat of butter over the entire cooking surface,
then cover with batter and raisins.
When the bottom begins to brown

like the farmer's freckles in the planting season, flip carefully.
As the other side cooks, break the pancake
into bite-sized pieces using a knife and spoon.
Serve with lemon sugar and the old world's grace,
an added dressing of melted butter optional.

for Mimi

lullaby

for X—who couldn't sleep without one

Dear Sir:

I know what your body holds for me—shame, oil and shame. When you first touched me it was like the morning of my seventh birthday when, in helping Grandmother prepare the cake, I cracked open an egg laid by our best hen only to watch a shell's worth of blood slip into the batter. That is to say I find your kisses dark and gelatinous. They ruin things. Do you know that on our daily walks while in your company I have never seen a bird? What powers you must possess to spirit away such beauty! I have heard tell the grocer's wife makes it known to all who would listen that last winter she observed you unaware in the cemetery, that you stood a full hour before the stone of your dearest mother who died in your inexorable birthing and that when, at the approach of dusk you turned to leave, your face was bathed with light, tears and light. I myself have heard the grocer's wife tell this very tale innumerable times, and with each telling I see you grow more and more the little pig of children's games. Yes, the comparison is apt—you are the little piggy who cried wee wee wee wee wee wee all the way home and I am the one who had none. Perhaps you know where this is going. I tell you of my revulsions not with any hope of forgiveness, but because I must.[1] I know now that you are not Satan's darkling but a man and a needy one at that. Sir, can you hear me? This is the oldest story we have. Your love is buried in the earth and by now has fallen to ash. Because my breasts were not made for such unholy thirsts, despite Genesis I would leave you as—

My Own Excision[2]

---

[1]True, true, these are the spinnings of my mind's dark helmet—fabrications, pejoratives and fabrications. (Let the record show there never was a daily walk, a best hen, tête-à-têtes with the neighbor's wife, etc.) You may ask who am I to write such puritanical obfuscations in the year nineteen hundred and ninety eight. I defend myself thusly: at times the bright lie makes a more honest truth. Or more accurately, I prefer the landscape.

[2]This is the pleasure of adopting a heightened rhetoric. While admittedly the atrocities detailed above are purely fictive in nature, the cathartic hysteria has allowed the speaker to arrive albeit late at an epiphanic moment in the text. Yes. It is now safe to say in plain speak sleep on this: I hate you for who you are and what you did.

lunar eclipse

Chiang Mai

Nobody knew it was coming.

Evening
we fell out of the river.
The elephants took us with them
because they had to. Some of us laughed.
The boy with the bamboo crop
said we were almost there. He smiled
like a flower, pressed and red.

In the village of the people
with the necks long as glass,
the children dancing for coins,
we spent all night thinking
of waterfalls, how summer's black razor
opened our faces.

Then we knew.
Like a soldier dying with a message.
The bloodspice, the smoke.
We saw pages of darkness.
The earth lay down
like a child in the road.
We spoke into our own mouths
and still they were shells of bones.

High in the Thai hills
a people wiped the caul
from the eye of their only god.
The how is a secret, the why
brought our conversion.
Fall on your knees. It's rising.

Out of the forest with its
trophy of hair.

maleficium

The Devil came to me and bid me serve him.
—Tituba at her 1692 examination

I. GENESIS

I tell the marrow only of truths. *A tall man*
In black clothes. The steeples of Boston
Hollow as skulls. Before
My days were filled with sugar. Before that,
With life. *We ride upon sticks and are there presently,*
Sails wimpled in idolatrous wind. What once was fed.

As always slavery is an institution of finery. Leisure.
Unnatural silence. What shouldn't survive.
Like a city on a hill or a commonwealth of swamps.
When He comes, the praying towns fall diseased
In a communicable reign of sores. I know what exists
Before the beginning, crawls shin over shin

From the thicket of ribs. Such suggestible maidens.
Now divining the manner of next days, separating
The beast from shell, gelatinous white from natal wing.
A box opens in water. Someone remembers
The covenant with good. It's breathing, *upright*
Like a man and wholly misunderstood.

He tells me he's God and I must believe him.
Here I was made; we lick toads to see spirits—
Even His. On this island, its killing floor
Stalked with sugar, I have awareness
Of what comes in threes. The death's first pustules.
Ships. Negroes stock cattle and utensils listed

On the deceased last voluntary act and deed.
Some marks red, some yellow, a great many.
I too am marked in his ledger—"Tattuba," adherent, slave.
I'm not even black. He gives me this name
And my soul stays with me. I become the feminine
Of us, a people thinned by an indigenous river.

Then I find myself bound for a winter of tongues, my new lord
Like a prophet and his staff—*a tall man with white hair*
Who won't let me go. The sloop like a heresy
Bearing us to fire. Against him and his, I couldn't intend
More. I say—even a threshold proscribed with blood
Won't keep him from knocking.

III. REVELATION

There will be others. *With white silk hoods.*
With topknots. Commonwealth of gallows.
I know what motivates them, such suggestible citizens
In a world of lords. The real crime is that so many
Felt deserving to die. After everything I did,
Me, the one who versed them in survival.

Is it really such an offense? To rejoice
Even in being kept? As is right, amnesty
Cloaks those who can afford its treatments.
I am the feminine of my nation, the ones traded
Like beads. Nobody knows my name,
Can decant my soul from its true appellation.

Now in the hour of omega,
One like a man comes as I am going to sleep.
My rightful master unburdens me. I swear on my life,
This dark leash the good people fastened. I want someone
To set it down. I was never alone.

masochism

after Lucie Brock-Broido

was the meek.
was montgomery overcome.

was bombed. was empty buses.
was bull's eye to bullet,

the billy club, the bloody church.
am black. historically

was skin kindling. was prey
to hook and hood. was the named thing

and never called. learned
to take a beating. was silent

despite the presentation of the throat,
the brick and truncheon,

the gutting clean. nineteen
fifty five and the we

walking there and back. was the seeing
of things for the first time, the tele-

vision, the web of fire.
opposed the politicians in the door,

the turning on of the dogs, the sicking
of the hoses. am the nonviolently

strong. was the women and children first.
was song. was the lifting out of egyptland.

was black eyes. was swollen lips. was asking for it.
the sitting down. the giving over.

Meanwhile, Back in the Relative Safety of a Ticker Tape Parade, Buzz Aldrin has a Moment of Epiphany . . .

Yes, the moon is made of gunpowder because that's how it smells—
the whole Sea of Tranquility's a CIA sham: it's really a loaded keg, miles
of galactic hotbeds waiting to blow those pinko commies off their asses
should they ever land one of these days & POW! right in the kisser
& then where will Comrade Khrushchev go? I keep the moondust
stored in a cool dry place in the third lobe of my right lung because
Neil keeps it there too, I can tell from his hot bronchial breath
that he's hoping to corner the market on this organic gunpowder thing, yeah
he told me as much over Madagascar when we crossed the terminator
into the cold cislunar night, the vacuum between heaven & hell/New York
City. I might add vacuum is no longer just a word to me like Rigel Fomalhaut Altair.
Holy mother of the eagle has landed! I was born here & I'll die here
against my will, against my will, I'm practically singing I'm so goddamn
full of earthshine—

night soil man

I.

All love is vascular. You pull
yourself out of earth's thighs, body
sullied with the body's rot, two heaping pails
steaming with profanity.

II.

It's post-war Japan. There are no cows.
Still thirty years from Kobé
and the beef famed for beer, massage
tenderizing as a fist in foreplay.

III.

Stark like the eyes of a dead fish
and as conscious. Your hands begin
a motion they've never been taught.
Even St. Sebastian converted among men.

IV.

Simply: to fertilize is to love
as feet are to gloves. You mine in drifts,
deeply, deeper. The ground's bowels shriek
like a duct cleansing itself of itself.

V.

When your wife comes to bed
smelling of lilac and soy, you picture her in
trousers, you desire her with each cuff
stained by subterfuge, the masculine weapon.

VI.

You remember everything about your birth—
the porcelain dish, the clasping light,
the first minerals passing through you,
dust to dust, like to seminal like.

oracle

Snakes don't lie.
You should have killed me
when you could.

Before the rain. Now
harboring your own death
like a feeding tick,

like a child.
Didn't you think I'd survive?
The night a wall of teeth,

the ocean's slow stew.
Daddy, I know how much blood
it takes to make life.

Open your chest to us. It's time.

plague

> There was a young man from Back Bay
> Who thought syphilis just went away.
> He believed that a chancre
> Was only a canker
> That healed in a week and a day.
> —anonymous

I. TREPONEMA PALLIDUM

After three weeks a chancre forms—an ulceration
with a hard edge, springy center—the way a button
feels through a layer of cloth. Also, the lymph nodes

in the groin begin distorting, swell like vulcanized rubber,
painless though immunologically ineffectual.
Week eight. The primary lesion sloughs down to a scar.

The host's hair combs out in patches, the body
a culture of warts, rashes, the mucous gray, moist
as snail tracks. In the secondary stage, ten percent

lapse into irritation, meningitis. Finally
one year after infection, after the pustules scab and flake,
remission—for some a permanent stay. For unknown reasons

in many of the untreated, the third stage fails to develop.
The skin never rots away, the skull is never kissed by light
as the brain shrinks, the spinal cord racked with *tabes dorsalis,*

shin pain said to feel as though someone were beating
        the legs with the back of an axe. No. Thirty-five years
            after the initial act, some lucky syphilitics

                never encounter the mental deterioration, concentration
        less and less, their emotional control slipping, the episodic
rages, the delusions of grandeur, of guilt.

II. SOMEWHERE

an unsuspecting man is walking you across a carpet.
Like a slave, you go where he goes, a white bacterium
coiled 20 mu, slipping by the thousands
through the membranous eye of a needle.
You know evolution, the descent of man
for what it truly is. Que será, será. Every day a gift.

Hitler. Dürer. Van Gogh. Nietzsche.
  Three popes, countless kings, which means

all their lascivious courts.
  Inspired by a rational phobia

of boils, Catherine the Great allegedly
  kept royal tasters—"les Epreuveuses," six women

assigned to venery, given two calendar seasons
  to diagnose those who would love a tzarina.

It's present in Cellini's casting of Perseus, the disembodied
  head still wriggling like a spirochete. In Keats's dame

sans merci, the warriors pale, enthralled.
  Schopenhauer found reasons to hate

just as Giovanni Casanova found reasons to otherwise.
  Caesar, Cleopatra. Abraham, his "sister" Sarah. Pharaoh,

Pharaoh's harem. Goya. Gauguin. Consequently Tahiti.
  The sometime Calvinist James Boswell bemoaning what he thought

was a "winter's safe copulation." Said one of the damned,
  "A man who does not have the pox

is not a polished gentleman." Said Don Columbus, back
  more than ten years, brain inflamed in the tertiary stage,

"I am God's Ambassador," his body dropsical
   like a ship filling with water, the bacteria ravenous as an empire

called forth, multiplying.

IV. TUSKEGEE

Somehow you do recall
it had a point. Fluid. Yours.
The white doctors
eager to draw blood,
tap the spine.
They said they needed it
just as it was—pristine.
All you remember
are months of headaches and the bloody crusts
that never went away, every summer
the doctors armed with needles.
How your children died at birth
or how they should have.
How much the state reimbursed you
for each black and boneless face.

post-partum

Just a month before she was to have become a mother, a young peasant
woman was carried away by a sudden illness to the Land of the Dead,
though the day after her burial she was spotted in the market.
—Vietnamese ghost tale

I tell you it is better this way.
I have taken the last coin from my eyes

and spent it on honey. The betel woman, her teeth
scarlet as the rooster's comb, is onto nothing

though her grandchild, the pretty one who hates
the old woman's dark spit, followed me

as I returned with my jar
of sweet light. I tell you they will come for you

in the evening. After the bell has called the women
from the fields. They will bring the men with torches

and with spades, and your father will place the bowl
of his ear to the ground and hear your long cry

trembling through the dirt. I tell you they will dig
for you, cracking the lid from this freshly laid box, pitch-sealed

and milkless. A woman will come forward, guide
your silt-caked head to her breast, and then the legend

of the child of death
will be born. Now as we wait, the tamarind fixed

above like stars, your mouth suckling
my honey-slicked fingers, I tell you

be her daughter. We had our chance.

reading

Ann Arbor

He just sat there
eating from the bowls of his hands.
When it was over the poets rushed out,
back into the bookjackets of their lives. He just sat quietly
warm in the droppings of words, belly full,
the complimentary wine rising in him. Outside
the long night waited to take him home.

Snow White

In some versions
he kisses me. In others

the glass coffin shatters,
the apple dislodges

its bruise from my throat.
However it happens,

he won't let me sleep—
this marital morning

the invasive clouds
festooned with ice.

some refrains Sam would have played had he been asked

You must remember nothing. Loyalty is as useless
as an assassination. Treaties broken like a night of glass.
I left Harlem to be my own man. Got shanghaied in Europe,
a theatre volatile as the moon. Pallid as a master race.

❧ ❧

You've always been good at the carving up.
Like a butcher with his canvas of meats hacking a landscape
through the offal. What gets burned. As Paris is learning,
the stratagem of black folk is to grin and resist.

❧ ❧

To you, rumors are like falling in love—not even as sound
as a spin of the wheel. Like the rising sun,
each atrocity millions of miles removed. How long
won't you believe? What you do to me they'll do to you.

❧ ❧

Even here in this city of a white house, you dream of clouds
sprouting like black lungs. Your love comes back
like a particle falling from a higher state. It's then you remember
every dog has his requited day. I'm still due.

❧ ❧

This is how it will end: a Japanese city named for an island
will beg for water. Each brown face adorned with the keloid star.
Even though you aren't sure, I know you have it in you. Ask my lord
if a kiss is just a kiss. Bwana, who's the boy now?

studio audience

Places everyone. The child star
darts in from the wings, game face hard

like a professional athlete
who doesn't have time to stop & think

tops I've only got two more seasons in me.
It's a half hour show, which means

twenty-three actual minutes of tape, the hook
formulated at fourteen minutes in then cut

to commercial. This is episode fifty-six:
"Two Green Thumbs." *Hijinks*

ensue as little Timmy learns a hard life lesson.
From seats rowed like lettuce

we know when to laugh, pay no attention
to the men behind the curtain

because the overhead sign cues us, our response
prompt as clocks. *Applause.*

A headsetted woman stands on-camera, snaps
the board shut, *scene 5 take 2*, wipe back

to Timmy & Principal Blop & the denouement
which predictably comes at the twenty spot.

If a tree falls in the forest & there's no key grip around . . .
But this is scripted. A functional TV family with Dolby sound

& body mics & TDs & four & five
takes, "home" a pasteboard set with out-of-shot signs flashing *live, live.*

synopsis

It's what's inside most folk that scares 'em.
—Clint Eastwood in *High Plains Drifter*

Finally, you paint the town red. You order up
two hundred gallons of crimson, one barbecued steer,
and tell the townspeople, "Get to work."
The local midget you've named mayor and sheriff

is on your side. He was hiding under the saloon on the night
you were bullwhipped to death by Stacey and his cousins.
They've just been released from jail
after serving one year for a crime they didn't commit.

This time it's personal. They plan to empty
the mining company's safe, dynamite the whole place
if it comes to that. Because of the paint, people, you rename
the town Hell. Now there is nothing to do but wait

for Stacey and his cousins to ride in. You find time
for exactly two forcible rapes, though the next morning
the women are seen radiantly combing their hair.
The midget mayor/sheriff asks when you'll give the signal.

You tell him, "I won't give the signal. You will."
High noon. Stacey and his cousins ride in
to find hoisted above the town's red square a banner
the local women have sewn together at your orders

with linen from the town's one red hotel. "Welcome home, boys!"
the banner says. In time Stacey and his cousins die
the kind of death men like Stacey and his cousins die.
Today the town is red and smoldering as are the women

who have acquired your taste. The midget mayor/sheriff
is busy with a knife. "I'm almost finished here," he pipes.
In last night's shoot out, he killed a man. "Finished," he says.
His handiwork is good. You take a last long look at Hell,

kick your horse in the ribs, tip your hat to the mayor/sheriff
and tell him through your teeth, "You knew it all along."

for Sean

tradition

My mother says   women were made to bleed
and the whole thing   takes twenty minutes.
She says afterwards   they'll wrap me up like a butterfly
for forty nights   and I'll drink only camel's milk.
My mother says   tomorrow
I'll be a little bride   hands red with henna.
I'll be shining in white   and get to wear as much gold
as I want. She says afterwards   something will get killed
and the whole clan   will come to eat
only they won't   sit down
until I've been washed   in the Nile.
My mother says tomorrow   the blacksmith's wife
will cut away a part of me   I don't need. She says
it might hurt   if the blacksmith's wife
uses scissors instead of a knife.   My sister says at her *khefad*
the blacksmith's wife used glass   and then tied her shut
with acacia thorns   and horsehair and Mother
had to remind her to put   a match head in the wound
so the whole thing   wouldn't heal closed
and my sister   could still pee.
My aunt says up north   they use something called cautery
which means they make that place   burn like the sun.
My mother says I have nothing   to fear
because women like us   were made to bleed.
My mother says someday   I'll meet a man
who'll want me smooth and small.   She says we'll marry
and he'll take a dagger   and slit me open
like a letter addressed   just to him.

My mother says tomorrow I'll   be a little bride. She says
the whole thing takes   twenty minutes
and after forty days   I'll come out just like her
smooth and small   lips sealed.

triage

> A gulf divides us, and there is no fairy bridge of birds to carry me across.

I. WHAT DUC SAID

For the most part, the small intestine is mine
as is the right hand and leg, the vena cava's dark pull

back to air. We share a bowel. A stump grows between us
like a radish so pale I suspect it shines when we sleep.

In your language you would say we are shaped like a T—
look closely and like the rain of airplanes

we will form before your eyes. Nights Viet dreams
of things north, of being left on mountains. Even the nurses

must learn to tolerate our form, our body wizened
like the burnt flocks that fall like a pogrom out of the sky.

II. WHAT VIET SAID

I don't like. To be alone.
When Duc sleeps. I feel our third leg shining.

Like the hare in the moon. Like a flare.
It casts our shadow on the ceiling. I fear it.

This dense cloud hanging. Over me.
Half of it is. Out of my control.

III. WHAT THEY SAID

there are things we know that we cannot say:
that she will not love as she should: that she will not die
when she wants: this is our beginning: she is walking
through the fields: the tall grains whisper

between her thighs: an early star: then
it is raining: the caustic drops sudden: sharp
as the braid that cuts the baby from its mother:
she thinks of rice: of seeds massing in the wind:

teratically the rain brings on a night that bleeds:
under the stiff white hare of the moon: on a path
raised like a scar: something inside her clicks
as if her body has pulled out the pin on 12 million:

this is the time we spend in the ellipse of our mother:
in the land of the seagull and fox: in a place
where a young girl will not love as she should:
will not die when she wants:

IV. WHAT SCIENCE SAID

"There were about 72 million litres of toxic chemicals
sprayed over Vietnamese land and Vietnamese people
during the war. This amount of toxic chemicals
was contaminated by 200–500 kilograms
of Dioxin (2•3•7•8 Tetra- Chloro-Debenzo-Para-Dioxin (TCDD))
contained in Agent Orange. An American scientist estimated that
only 85 grams of 2•3•7•8 TCDD
can kill all 12 million citizens of New York City."

V. WHAT I SAID

By conservative estimates the mangroves will not return
in this century. Neither will the eyes, the limbs twisted like roots.

Today Viet lies deep in the mosquito sickness—if he dies,
Duc dies too. There will be no time for separation, no time to airlift

the split being into surgery. Instead, the living half will wait passively
for what invariably will come rolling on, the roofs filling with people.

I didn't ask to survive.

"'Twas mercy brought me from my *Pagan* land"

> The compositions published under her name are below the dignity of
> criticism.
> —Thomas Jefferson

In your first winter you will be pronounced
Seven. Someone will pay to name you
For a ship. You will owe your life
To tight packing, the hull racing to port, human cargo

Impacted like teeth. Within months the floes
Will dissipate, the thaw freeing
The harbor's dark trade. You will master the spoken
Word, then Euclidian principles, then history,

Then the systems of the night sky, Latin
And the Bible falling as well. Finally
You will write. You will have paper
At your bed and keep a log burning

Through the prodigal darkness.
Only once will you speak of your mother's
Genuflecting at the sun. You will be carted
From sitting room to room. You will be a thing of wonder.

Generals will write your name. *Phillis. Phyllis.*
Like the colonies you too will come and go.

vigil

> And both the girls cried bitterly (though they hardly knew why) and clung
> to the Lion and kissed his mane and his nose and his paws and his great,
> sad eyes. Then he turned from them and walked out onto the top of the
> hill. And Lucy and Susan, crouching in the bushes, looked after him and
> this is what they saw.
> —C. S. Lewis, *The Lion, the Witch, and the Wardrobe*

Tonight we will function like women.
The snow has gone away, the ice with its amniotic glare.
I clasp my sister's tiny hand.
We will not turn away
Though spring, spring with its black appetite,
Comes seeping out of the earth.

The lion was sad. He suffered us
To touch him. When I placed the bread of my hands
In his mammalian heat, I was reminded
That the world outside this world
Is all vinegar and gall, that to be a young girl at the foot of a god
Requires patience. Timing.

The White Witch has mustered her partisans.
Because I am fascinated by her bracelets strung with baby teeth,
I will remember her as the woman
Who grins with her wrists. From my thicket of heather
I note that in her own congenital way
She is pure, that tonight she ushers something new into the world.

I cannot stop it. I cannot stop it just as in that other place
I could not keep the planes with their spiked fires from coming.
Though in this closed realm the smell of camphor is overwhelming
I have nothing but my hands to use
In ministering to the dead. Here too
My hands must suffice.

Hush now while I testify. They are shaving him.
The corona of his mane falls away
Like pieces of money. In the moon's milk light
Her bangled wrists grin as she raises the blade.
Something is diffused. In whatever world he comes again
There will be women like us who choose to.

visitor

In hindsight the amazing thing wasn't her surviving
but the fact that a stranger entered her room.

Of course it's all supposition, nothing
too convicting. Perhaps they struggled.

Maybe he simply ordered her supine.
All they uncovered: a locked house, her bedroom door

slightly ajar, approximately four pints staining
her pillow, a one inch section atop the crown of her head

crushed as finely as herbs. Three days later
the paperweight came back from the lab

sticky with an unreadable palm, almost as if
someone were cupping it, racing to beat

a stack of papers before they stirred.
I'm not making this up. She was my sister's best friend,

a teen with more than a hundred sutures
embedded in her scalp. Like a dead tree she went on,

maintaining she remembered nothing
about the incident, each night

sleeping behind the same door
across from his, desperate to believe

in the official version, in planned randomness.
I can't tell you her name. I won't tell you

because it's all you'll remember, you'll lie down at night
thinking it doesn't apply.

Whitsunday

Everything that will ever happen has happened.
The scorpion sheds its dead cardiac light, the southern cross
burns its orienting pall on the world.
Even the moon of the green corn slants her grained face
at a redundant angle. Behold! The sky is black with old news
and each year the earth spins itself through the same six seasons.
Do you know who I am? Or should I say, "Do you accept?"
This afternoon my god wrote his name on my skin, the flesh abraded,
salt-white and million-eyed. Reader, my god is a god of love—
he is studded with stinging arms. He grants me iridescence,
second sight: everything I will ever be I have been. Behold!
The scorpion sheds its red thoracic eye, the southern cross
burns its pall on the world. Night. Glory. Corn. Lord.
Isn't it enough my whole body tastes white?

Whitsunday

Today on land a lesser being would robe itself in glass.
Instead you give birth to yourself—the planulae, the polyps
budding five thousand times, pulsing through the ocean
like bright ventricles. What is it about the power of seven?
I was alone and you came to me, I was bleeding
and the blurred thumbprints of your eyes sensed it.
I would say I was in love with you, with your munificent power
to divide. Your kingdom is briny and many-tongued;
it is a forest at the bottom of the sea. I was alone and you came
to me, I was bleeding and you flashed your lobed impassive face,
the cilia of your raiment like glass, each vitric whip signifying:
"On this day a ladder of blood came down from the sky."
Why? Why adore you from this gray distance?
Put your hands on me. Make me writhe in your salt and fire.

Whitsunday

I wrote my own vows:
the ocean azure like a sky
filled with contrasts.
I wrote: *This time I want*
to be born right.
I wrote: *Death to tribulation.*
"Your robe suits me
like a ladder without rungs," I mean
"I'll always love you
like a spider," I mean—
damn this iridescence
in my mouth!
Why do you
twist my words?

Whitsunday

All I wanted was an island—
salt-white, aquamarine,
the forests crenulated and fern-dense,
the night scorpion-centered.
By the light of the green corn moon
you'd come to me
crossing the ocean on a white skiff,
each of your stinging arms munificent.
All I wanted was this place of glory
and things that can never be
to be. The sky is black, the southern cross
merciless. How I wanted to be born right.
Winter. Spring. Sorrow. Endeavor.
Fuck white. You started this.

woman in love/Agatha, doubting

Just say the word and I'll let myself
be led into the red humiliating light, ask

and I'll root through hot coals,
broken plates, I'll shut the rack's iron cuffs

on my own feet, use my teeth to tie my wrists
to the breaking point. I'd advance the wheel on myself

smashing the long icicle of my back
if I thought You'd be pleased.

Note this: I've come to You
bearing the stumps of my breasts arranged on a platter—

they are like two loaves of bread, they are like dark bells
tolling in Your hands—

what do I have to do?

zeitgeist

or Chapter VIII: The Death of the Poet

after *Red Pomegranate*

1.

One by one the men remove their black cassocks, let in the dawn.

2.

At the top of the stairs a door opens. Behind it, the darkness tactile, felt-like.

3.

She arrives in a green gilded gown, on her shoulder a white bird
    perched like a balance.

4.

If you touched them, the walls would crumble in your hands.

5.

The roof is made of stone. One by one the men unrobe. Even here
    they cry like candles.

6.

When someone speaks, it is only to command you to sing.

7.

What does it mean to fall on your knees, to let what spills from the jug

8.

Sing.

9.

pour over you?

10.

"Though I die, no more will be lost to the world."

11.

12.

Your sentence is an unpaved road. The fruit was bleeding.
    The camera never moves.

EPILOGUE

"Who lit this flame in us?"

I can say there are creatures that live on steam, there are flowers
that cast themselves in glass. Even now there is a manta ray
floating like a blank page, its body cartilaginous, a single wing
rippling. There are worlds within worlds within the tunics of the eye
and for each there are seven exits. All night there is
the song of the meniscus, all night the processes drift
here and back.

"I want to stay changeless for you."

Where is it written that we should want to be saved?
What did the water feel like? Where did constancy go?
How did the light fall through the trees?
In serrations? In flat bands?
What part said, "I don't want to have to."
What didn't you say? How did the earth respond?
When did you realize? Who let loose the shattering?

"If I don't meet you in this life, let me feel the lack."

Now there is almost no sound and at night I am not afraid.
The next world will be made of paper and everything
will have the capacity to fly. Promise me it will be there
as it is here—the raspberries climbing the trellis, the rivers
blue scripts. Because every story has two endings, I see your body
breaking down, I see you soaring in the light. Be taken with me.
Come pouring down unified.

"Who are you to live in all these many forms?"

There was another time, the duck's severed head
floating in the lagoon. I remember the canoe's broad balance,
how my dog crawled up on the floating island and I cried
because I didn't want her to sink through. How I came to realize
there are places where the earth goes unattached,
and how some things are light enough to walk there.
How nothing comes back, the wildflowers matted in their fur.

acknowledgments

Grateful acknowledgment is made to the Wallace E. Stegner Fellowship Program at Stanford University for its support in the writing of this manuscript. I would also like to thank the University of Wisconsin's Institute for Creative Writing for its generous Diane Middlebrook Poetry Fellowship (as well as its friendship) which has also been crucial in the formation of this work. Finally, I would like to acknowledge the following publications in which these poems first appeared:

The Missouri Review: "child of the enemy," "intermurals," "Whitsunday" ("Everything that has ever happened has happened"), "Whitsunday" ("Today on land, a lesser being would robe itself in glass"), "Who lit this flame in us?" and "If I don't meet you in this life, let me feel the lack."; *The New Yorker*: "If $dy/dx=4x^3 + x^2 - 12/ 2x^2 - 9$, then "; *P.N. Review* (U.K.): "asylum"

P J Harvey lyrics are from the song "To Bring You My Love" from the album of the same name, released in February 1995 by Island Records. In the poem " Meanwhile, Back in the Relative Safety of a Ticker Tape Parade, Buzz Aldrin has a Moment of Epiphany . . . " the line "I was born here and I'll die here against my will" is from the Bob Dylan song "Not Dark Yet," from the album *Time Out of Mind,* released in 1997 by Sony Music. The titles "Who lit this flame in us?" "I want to stay changeless for you," "If I don't meet you in this life, let me feel the lack," and "Who are you to live in all these many forms?" are quotes from the film *The Thin Red Line* by Phoenix Pictures and Fox 2000 Pictures.